HARLEY-DAVIDSON®
The Legend

HARLEY-DAVIDSON®
The Legend

Mac McDiarmid

SMITHMARK

Page 1: Symphony in chrome: no matter how hard the factory tries, no Harley is finished without an owner's extra touches. Page 2: Possibly the most evocative model name in motorcycling: a 1995 Electra Glide . . . Page 3: . . . and the first of the breed, an exquisite 1965 FL Panhead Electra Glide.

Figures and data in this book are generally quoted in Imperial measurements first, with the metric equivalents noted in brackets, where appropriate.

This edition published in 1998 by SMITHMARK Publishers, a division of U.S. Media Holdings, Inc., 115 West 18th Street, New York, NY 10011.

SMITHMARK books are available for bulk purchase for sales promotion and premium use. For details write or call the manager of special sales, SMITHMARK Publishers, 115 West 18th Street, New York, NY 10011.

Produced by Parragon
Units 13-17, Avonbridge Trading Estate, Atlantic Road,
Avonmouth, Bristol BS11 9QD United Kingdom

ISBN 0-7651-0848-8

Designed and produced by Touchstone

Printed in Italy
10 9 8 7 6 5 4 3 2 1

Photographic credits:
All photographs by **Mac McDiarmid** except:

EMAP (Classic Bike/Classic Motorcycle): 9, 12 (*below*), 14 (*below*), 18, 19, 24, 25 (*main picture*), 31, 40, 41.

Harley-Davidson: 8, 10, 13, 20 (*left*), 48, 49, 50, 51, 53 (*top*), 56 (top), 57, 59 (*left*), 65 (*top*), 66, 67, 68, 69.

With thanks to Jeremy Pick of Harley-Davidson UK Ltd for his assistance.

Andrew Morland: 6, 7 (*top*), 11, 14 (*top*), 25 (*top*), 29, 38, 44.

Contents

Introduction

THE Harley-Davidson Motor Company has better claims than most to be a motorcycling legend. True legends are old, and Harley has more history than most. No other motorcycle factory still in existence can trace continuous roots as far back as 1903, when the first Hog was born in a tiny wooden shed in America's Mid-West.

The city was Milwaukee, made famous, according to the song, by beer. But ask almost anyone, anywhere in the world, to name a make of motorcycle, and the chances are they'd reply 'Harley-Davidson' and know where it was made.

For Harleys have become more than mere motorcycles. It's almost impossible to switch on a TV set these days and not see a piece of Milwaukee iron shimmering in the make-believe of some advertising director's imagination. Harleys have been used to sell clothing, beer, perfume, holidays and just about anything else you can imagine – even cars. That's because just about every company which sells anything would like their product to be as evocative and familiar as the Harley-Davidson motorcycle. In this case, imitation truly is the sincerest form of flattery.

So Harleys are up there with Coca-Cola, Zippo lighters and Levi jeans on top of the 'instantly recognizable' scale. To some extent, it has to be said, they have accomplished this despite themselves. Although, like most motorcycle manufacturers, their early years brought a deal of innovation, most of the company's life has seen them producing technically outdated models which were far outstripped by their rivals.

Below: The classic side-valve 'flathead' Harley, a 1943 747cc WLC model, sturdy civilian cousin to the machines which powered America's war effort.

For many years the same lack of imagination characterized Harley's marketing. This was to bring them to the brink of collapse little more than a decade ago. It took the intervention of President Reagan to help the company survive. But then, if you're a national treasure, you tend to have friends in high places.

And then something remarkable happened. A new management set about not only the long-overdue refinement of their models (but nothing too radical, you understand . . .), and at the same time began to exploit the priceless 'All American' image the company's products had already secured.

Above: Launched in 1936, the Knucklehead was the first volume-production overhead valve V-twin, a layout it shares with the modern Electra Glide (right).

The initiative was bold and slick, and struck a chord in the public imagination.

Harley have never looked back. Today they make more machines annually than ever before, yet can sell every motorcycle they produce two times over. Harleys are expensive, yet hold their value better than any other make of motorcycle. There is a very good reason for this: all Harleys are precious. But of course: they are legends, after all.

The Birth Of An American Eagle

THE Eagle began hatching around 1901, when William S. Harley and Arthur Davidson began messing about in a Milwaukee basement workshop. Harley, 21, worked as a draughtsman; Davidson, a year his junior, was a pattern maker with the same firm, Barth Manufacturing. A German colleague was familiar with pioneering European motorcycles, an influence which helped fire the founders' enthusiasm. They roped in two other Davidson brothers to their project: Walter and, a couple of years later, William A.

Their first machine was designed by Bill and hand-made by Walter from Art's drawings. Legend has it that the first carburettor was made from a discarded tomato can. A single cylinder contraption of 10cu in (161cc), it didn't so much scream as twitter, feebly. Later, when bored and stroked to 25 cu in. (410cc) and with help in carburettor design from Ole Evinrude (later to find fame with his outboard motors), it pushed out just three horsepower – so few that it was pedal-assisted, like a moped.

In 1903 – the year the Wright brothers took to the air – Harley-Davidson produced a single machine in a wooden shed measuring 10 feet by 15 (3 x 4.5m) built in the Davidson back yard by Davidson senior, a cabinet maker. The following year they built a further two bikes, of a model later nicknamed the 'Silent Grey Fellow', the first of which was sold to a gentleman name Meyer. The machine's humble name doesn't exactly get the adrenaline flowing in the 1990s. Yet they clearly got something right: ten years later they were advertising that one of these had travelled 100,000 miles (161,000km) on its original bearings.

In their second full year, working part-time, Harley-D's founders built no less than eight machines, all 28cu in (440cc) Model 4s, producing fractionally less than four horsepower. Two years later production moved from 38th and Highway Boulevard into their first building on the present Juneau Avenue site. The new factory turned out to be partially built on land belonging to the adjacent railroad. Fortunately it measured only 28 x 80 feet (8.5 x 24m), and was light enough for ten men to pick up and carry to its proper location. Finance for the development had come from James McLay, a relative of the founders; from his hobby of beekeeping he became affectionately known as 'the honey uncle'.

This affectionate tribute was more appropriate than the founders were aware for Juneau Avenue was now a veritable hive of activity, seven days a week, 365 days in the year. Amateurish enthusiasm was giving way to conscientious professionalism. Harley-Davidson was on its way.

Below: The first Harley 'factory', on the Juneau Avenue site they occupy still, was light enough to be carried by ten men.

MODEL NUMBERS

Harley appear always to have favoured a particularly cryptic method of model designation, although the system is in most cases quite simple once the 'code' is understood. The first model made in any significant numbers was the Model 4 of 1908. The Model 5 followed in 1909, the Model 6 in 1910, and so on, until all models adopted the last two digits of their year of manufacture in 1916 (Model 16).

All machines produced in any year shared the same numerical prefix, with one or more letter added to denote type. Thus, a Model 6 was the basic 1910 single, whilst a 6A was the same with magneto ignition and a 6D was a 1910 twin. Later, as the range became almost entirely composed of V-twins, the suffix letters became more elaborate and numerous. An explanation of model codes can be found on page 56.

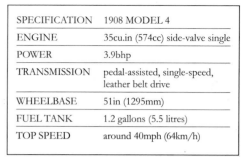

SPECIFICATION	1908 MODEL 4
ENGINE	35cu.in (574cc) side-valve single
POWER	3.9bhp
TRANSMISSION	pedal-assisted, single-speed, leather belt drive
WHEELBASE	51in (1295mm)
FUEL TANK	1.2 gallons (5.5 litres)
TOP SPEED	around 40mph (64km/h)

Below: In 1903 the first Harley-Davidson model, nicknamed 'the Silent Gray Fellow', produced just 3hp from its 25cu.in (410cc). The engine was single-speed, driving the rear wheel directly by leather belt. The engine was later enlarged to 35cu.in (574cc) by increasing the bore, offering an additional one horsepower.

9

The First Twins

IN 1907 the company was getting serious: it became Harley-Davidson Inc., and sold the first of what would be many thousands of machines for police duty. They had already taken on extra staff; William Harley had begun an engineering degree at the University of Wisconsin in Madison; Walter was getting into the mysteries of the heat treatment of metals; and the enterprise, with Arthur as company secretary and sales manager, was beginning to take a more professional approach to production and training. They may have begun as four young men with more enthusiasm than talent, but they had ambitions for the company they had created. That year they produced no less than 150 machines.

Even so, it was clear that further progress demanded a more ambitious new motorcycle than the existing single. In 1908 William graduated, and began the design of a more potent engine. This bore fruit a year later with the launch of Harley's first V-twin, the Model '5D', essentially a doubled-up single with strengthened bottom-end. A side-valve design of 49.5 cubic inches (811cc), it was rated at 6.5 horsepower, capable of propelling it to a top speed of 60mph (97km/h). The cylinders were splayed at the same 45 degree angle as are today's Harleys. There were early valvegear problems – production ceased during 1910 whilst these were sorted out – but eventually the V-twin's

assets of ease of manufacture, slim dimensions and punchy power (in an age of primitive transmissions) was to make it the mainstay of US motorcycling, not only for Harley but for a host of lesser-known manufacturers as well.

During 1908 production from the rapidly expanding company soared to 450 machines. The new, brick-built factory now occupied 2380 square feet (222m²), in which 18 men were employed. New machinery arrived almost weekly, and was set to work, according to legend, 'as soon as the cement was dry'.

In June of the same year, Walter took one of his bikes to its first competition success, a two-day endurance run in New York's Catskill Mountains. The sole Harley scored a 'perfect' 1000 points, outstripping all the more fancied runners in a field of 61 machines. In July Walter struck comparable success in a Long Island economy run, achieving no less than 188mpg (80km/lit) over 50 miles (80km).

Despite this success, for several years the factory resisted official racing, even when a private owner took the new 61-inch (1000cc) X8E twin (the first Harley with a real clutch) to victory in the 1912 San Jose road race by no less than 17 miles (27km). Two years later Bill Harley established a works race department.

By the time the new 5-35 single (the designation indicated 5hp-35cu in) appeared in 1913, the company had established a country-wide reputation for producing machines which were

Left: They may not look prepossessing, but they founded a legend. From left to right: Arthur Davidson, Walter Davidson, William S. Harley and William Davidson.

dependable in everyday as well as competition use. By now production had mushroomed to 13,000 motorcycles per year in a facility measuring 297,000 square feet (27,600m²). But it was not to be long before both factors were summoned by Uncle Sam.

Left and Below: From 1912 the original 49cu.in (811cc) V-twin was available with a capacity of 61cu.in (989cc) twin, as in this handsome 1915 Model 11F.

SPECIFICATION	1911 MODEL 7D
ENGINE	49.48cu.in (811cc) side-valve 45 degree V-twin
POWER	6.5bhp
TRANSMISSION	single-speed, leather belt drive
WHEELBASE	56.5in (1435mm)
FUEL TANK	2.0 gallons (9.1 litres)
TOP SPEED	around 60mph (97km/h)

Cruisin' With Uncle Sam

IN THE years preceding the First World War, Harley had maintained a steady stream of technical innovations. As early as 1912 they had offered a choice of coil or magneto ignition; in 1911, an advanced roller chain transmission and 'F-head' layout (overhead inlet valve, side exhaust valve). 1914 brought an early sort of kick-start ('step-starting'), the carburettor choke, internally-expanding rear drum brakes, and two-speed transmission. The first three-speed Harley appeared the following year.

The factory, too, was hurtling ahead. Now, over 1500 employees worked for a company whose manufacturing floor area had grown from 150 to almost 300,000 square feet (14 to 27,870m²) in little more than a decade. Production had rocketed from eight machines in 1905, to 1,149 in 1909 and 17,439

in 1916, the year prior to war. Bill Harley's competition department was also vigorously up-and-running, posting 26 major wins in its first year of operation.

In 1917 America's declaration of war with Germany demanded a more utilitarian approach, and Harley-Davidson were up to the task. Their machines had already seen military action in border skirmishes with the forces of Pancho Villa, the Mexican revolutionary.

Left: A new range of two-speed singles known as the 5-35 series, appeared in 1913. The figures stood for five horsepower and 35cu.in. This is a 1914 model 10.

SPECIFICATION	5-35, 1913-1918
ENGINE	30.17cu.in (494cc)
POWER	around 5bhp
TRANSMISSION	2-speed with clutch (1914-on, 3-speed 1915-on), chain drive
WHEELBASE	56.5in (1435mm)
FUEL TANK	2.0 gallons (9.1 litres)
TOP SPEED	around 55mph (89km/h)

Left: William S. Harley (in bowler hat) inspects Harleys with unusual custom accessories during the First World War. Around 20,000 Harley-Davidsons, mainly 61cu.in (989cc) side-valve V-twins, reached the American forces. Despite the armoury pictured here, most were used for despatch duties.
Below: Early sidecars were deeply unladylike, but by 1913 wicker-bodied devices such as this had arrived from Britain to broaden the appeal of motorcycling.

13

In all some 20,000 motorcycles became American 'conscripts' in the First World War, the vast majority of which were Harley-Davidsons. Mainly of conventional side-valve design, producing almost nine horsepower from their 60.34cu in (988cc), they were employed mainly for despatch and scout duty. One, however, became a *cause célèbre*.

On 8th November 1918, with the German army in chaotic retreat, Corporal Roy Holtz was assigned to take his commander on a mission. At night and in foul weather, the duo became lost and stumbled upon an enemy field headquarters. They were taken prisoner but released with the armistice three days later. Holtz – and his Harley V-twin – were thus credited with being the first American servicemen on German soil.

Anecdotes aside, the War had done little to harm Harley's commercial prospects. With rival European motorcycle manufacturers preoccupied by hostilities for a much longer period (1914-18), Milwaukee was able to extend its markets overseas, an advantage it has strived to maintain ever since. By 1918 Harley-Davidson was the world's largest manufacturer of motorcycles.

Another legacy of war, oddly, was colour. For some reason Harley persisted with the 'army green' which had replaced the traditional grey during the conflict until forced to brighten up their image by the catastrophic slump of the Thirties. It was in this livery that the first major new model of the post-war era emerged. Odder still, it was not a V-twin.

Roaring Into The Twenties

THE Model W Sport Twin unveiled as peace returned in 1919 was unique among Harleys – or indeed American motorcycles in general. Instead of the vee layout, the 37-inch (600cc) twin adopted a horizontally opposed design, similar in type to today's BMWs. But instead of lying across the frame, the cylinders were orientated fore-and-aft, much in the manner of pre-war British Douglas machines. Although long and unwieldy, the layout offered a very low centre of gravity and a compact width, ideally suited to the crude road network of the time.

There were other innovations, most of which would stand the test of time better than the model itself. The final drive was sensibly protected from dust in a metal enclosure, not unlike more recent MZ two-stroke machines. It was also the first model to feature a full electrical system produced by the Harley factory. Although the revvy little Sport set many records – not least Canada to Mexico in a mere 65 hours, no easy task even today – it lacked the bottomless big-inch power America demanded and was discontinued after 1922.

Part of the reason for this was the trade recession of 1920, and the efforts of a Mr Henry Ford to produce motor cars almost as cheaply as motorcycles. The trade slump was brief, but

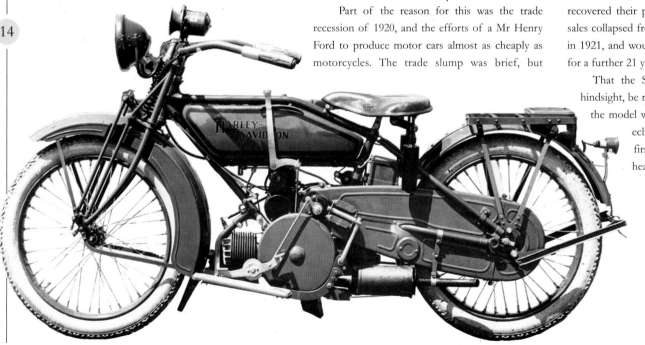

America's love affair with the car was not, and neither Harley nor any other manufacturer fully recovered their previous momentum. Milwaukee's sales collapsed from over 28,000 in 1920 to 10,202 in 1921, and would not recover to the 1920 figure for a further 21 years.

That the Sport's demise should not, with hindsight, be regarded as a loss is entirely due to the model which superseded it. 1921 saw the eclipse of the 61-inch V-twin by the first 74-inch (1200cc) model, with 'L-head' pocket valve layout. Dubbed

Left: In 1919 an unusual Harley appeared, the lightweight flat twin Model W. Intended as a sporting alternative to the earlier singles, it was not a success, and was dropped in 1922. Above: Customers preferred simple singles, or the lustier beat of a big V-twin.

14

the 'Superpowered Twin' (but commonly called the 'JD', which was, strictly, only the generator-equipped version), it traces its descent to today's 80-inchers. In 1930 it regressed to a side-valve format (albeit with heads designed by the great Harry Ricardo) as the 30V and VL (L: high compression) Big Twins which, after embarrassing early problems with engine, transmission and even frames, became staple models for a decade.

As to the rest of the range, the 30-inch (490cc) single had been dropped after 1918. In 1926 a new single, the 21-inch (350cc) Model A was introduced, to be joined four years later by a 30.5-inch (492cc). In '28 Harley got radical and pioneered the front brake, as they had pioneered kick-starts and three-speed transmissions over a decade earlier.

All models were sold in varied specifications of transmission, valvegear and power so that in 1928, for instance, three basic engine types accounted for no less than a dozen models. A year later still, a new 45-inch (737cc) side-valve V-twin arrived. It was of humble origins, but it was to become an American legend in its own right.

Above: The V-engine which replaced the Model W was the immortal 'JD', the 'Superpowered Twin'. It continued almost unchanged through the 1920s, at prices as low as $360.

SPECIFICATION	JD/FD
ENGINE	74cu.in (1207cc) 'L-head' V-twin
POWER	18bhp
TRANSMISSION	3-speed, all chain drive
WHEELBASE	59.5in (1511mm)
FUEL TANK	2.6 gallons (11.8 litres)
TOP SPEED	around 68mph (109km/h)

WL45: The Old Soldier

IF Harley-Davidson is the most enduring of all motorcycle companies, the 45cu in (750cc) sidevalver is probably their longest-lasting model. The humble side-valve V-twin began life as the Model D in 1929, continuing in production with only relatively minor modifications until the arrival of the 'K' Model in 1952. Indeed much the same engine powered Harley's peculiar Servi-Car trike until 1974. For an entire generation, this was *the* Harley-Davidson, as American as apple pie.

This was the first of a new generation of side-valve 'flathead' V-twins, for in 1930 it was joined by the 74-inch (1200cc) VL. Peak output of the 750cc twin was some 25 horsepower at 4500rpm. But it was the indefatigable manner with which the twin produced this power that really attracted attention. So confident were Harley of its success, that even in the first year of manufacture, three versions were produced: the low-compression D (also with a sidecar variant); the higher-compression DL and the 'Special Sport Solo' DLD.

In 1934 it was re-designated Model R, before being revamped and re-named again in '36. The Model W, as it was then known, benefited from much-improved lubrication, and the designation 'W' duly replaced the original 'D'. Plain W indicated a low-compression version, whilst WL was standard, WLD high compression, WLDR competition-spec and WS meant sidecar gearing. Later WLAs were designed for military use. All shared the same bullet-proof virtues. So, although more advanced models followed, the WL plodded doggedly on, its girder forks, side-valve engine and rigid rear end a growing anachronism, but its sheer indestructibility continuing to be prized.

The WL is – and was for most of its life – a crude, heavy machine better suited to the American prairies than any road with bends. Cruising all day at 60mph (96km/h) on a long, straight road, it is in its element. But with 550lb (250kg) of momentum, poor brakes, minimal suspension and a wide gap between its three gear ratios, anything else is hard work. Even setting off is a knack, thanks to the WL's hand gearchange and foot-operated 'suicide' clutch.

Long before it bowed out in 1952 the WL was already a motorcycling dinosaur. But although it was slow, outdated and cumbersome, it worked: strong as an ox and almost indestructible, a tough old workhorse that delivered the bacon. It would take something special to replace it, and it did: the K model not only featured hydraulically damped suspension at both ends, but was later to develop into a legend in its own right: the Sportster.

Right: On the principle that 'if it ain't broke, don't fix it', Harley rarely changed anything in a hurry. By 1936 the immortal WL had evolved from the Model D and Model R, and in the design of its crankcases can be seen clear echoes of the later Knucklehead and Panhead engines. Thousands of military versions of the side-valve twin – the WLA – served with distinction during the Second World War.

16

SPECIFICATION	WL45
ENGINE	45.32cu.in (743cc) side-valve V-twin
POWER	up to 24.5bhp @ 4600rpm
TRANSMISSION	3-speed
WHEELBASE	56.5in (1435mm)
FUEL TANK	3.0 gallons (13.6 litres)
WEIGHT (dry)	550lb (249kg)
TOP SPEED	around 70mph (113km/h)

17

Survival Of The Fittest

IN THE prosperous Twenties President Calvin Coolidge had declared that 'the business of America is business', a sentiment which had seen Harley-Davidson rise to pre-eminence in US motorcycle production. Yet following the Wall Street crash of October 1929 the American economy went into rapid reverse.

By 1933 one quarter of the US workforce was unemployed. Very few people had money to spend on motorcycles. Of literally hundreds of American bike manufacturers, only Harley and Indian had the financial strength and acumen to survive as industry-wide production plummeted from 32,000 to 6000 units per year in 1933, by which time fewer than 100,000 motorcycles were registered in the

whole of the USA. Of these new sales, Milwaukee's share was just 3,703 – their lowest for 23 years.

The most ironic Harley response came in 1932 with the licensing of Harley production to Japan under the Rikuo name. More conventionally – and certainly more enduringly – was the sale of branded clothing and accessories, a 'side-line' now worth millions of dollars per year. Perhaps the most apparently superficial but actually significant

measure was the abandonment in 1933 of dull green paint in favour of more vivid colours and art deco graphics which continue to brighten Harley-Davidsons today. Then there was the three-wheeled 'Servi-Car', a cheap delivery and police vehicle powered by the 45-inch (750cc) Model D engine.

Surprisingly, given the fraught circumstances of the time, this three-wheeler was both a sound design and a solid piece of engineering – so tough and enduring, indeed, that it survived in production from 1932 until 1974 (from 1934 with reverse gear and from 1936 with the improved Model W engine). Some were still in service with American police

Below: The 74cu.in (1208cc) VL introduced in 1930 never fully recovered from early teething troubles. By the time this example was built in 1936, art deco graphics were attempting to lure buyers.

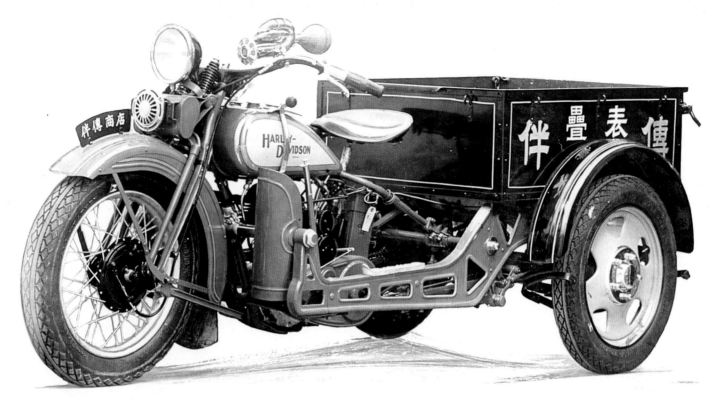

forces well into the Nineties. One clever and user-friendly touch was the adoption of the same 42 inch (1067mm) track as the typical car – inexperienced Servi-Car drivers would not need to forge their own ruts in mud and snow.

But if these tactics helped pull Harley out of an economic rut, the true hero of the Depression years was the good ol' side-valve twin: cheap to produce, economic to run and maintain, able to be fixed with whatever happened to be lying around.

Almost on their own, the DL and later WL and VL models saw Harley through this ordeal, along with a new 30.5-inch (500cc) single-cylinder machine to augment the existing 21-incher. As the financial vice tightened, no other significant new models were to be developed during six years of economic strife.

The worst of the Depression also brought out the best in Harley-Davidson, the company. By reducing the length of the working week, as many staff were kept in work as possible – a less altruistic measure than it might appear, since it was partially mandated by the government's National Recovery Administration, and every skilled hand would be needed when the slump finally abated. Somehow, even in the worst sales year, Juneau Avenue managed to turn a small profit. Prudent financial controls, police and military contracts, novel sales strategies and energetic pursuit of exports kept the company afloat, but it was a close-run thing.

Above: Despite its weird appearance, the Servi-Car proved ideal for the depression-hit Thirties market. Powered by the 45cu.in (743cc) side-valve V-twin unit, the trike proved marvellously versatile and robust, continuing in production from 1932 until well into the Seventies.

SPECIFICATION	VL, 1930-1940
ENGINE	74cu.in (1207cc) side-valve V-twin
POWER	25bhp
TRANSMISSION	3-speed
WHEELBASE	60in (1524mm)
FUEL TANK	3.2 gallons (14.6 litres)
TOP SPEED	around 76mph (122km/h)

The Knucklehead Years

SLOWLY but surely the crippling Depression came to a close. But it was not until 1936 when President Roosevelt's 'New Deal' began really to bite that new models began to emerge, for only two basic models had figured in Milwaukee's 1935 range. These were the 45-inch (750cc) Model R, soon to become the heroic Model W; and the 74-inch (1200cc) Model V and its derivatives, now fully cured of its original and varied ills. But both were side-valve designs, slow and steady, whereas the American public increasingly craved more advanced machines.

The biggest newcomer was the V-twin Model UL. Although still side-valve and visually similar to the proven DL45, this behemoth displaced a stupendous 80cu in (1340cc), making it ideal for heavy sidecar use. It was to continue in production until 1945. But most important of all was a new generation of 61-inch (1000cc) twin with overhead valves and twice the power of the '61' it eclipsed. The legendary Knucklehead had arrived.

Getting the Knuckle into the shops had been a frustrating experience for Harley. But for government restrictions aimed at reducing employment, it would probably have arrived in 1934. But it was certainly worth the wait. The Knuckle was a Juneau Avenue 'first' in many respects – first four (forward) speeder, first overhead valve, first hemispherical heads. The engine was heavily influenced by the competition experience of the legendary Joe Petrali, a Harley development rider and near-unbeatable racer. It duly announced its arrival by posting 136.183mph (219.12km/h) on the sands of Daytona Beach, Florida. The rider, naturally, was Joe, and his waterside speed record stands to this day.

With the new model as its flagship, Harley's fortunes rapidly improved. In 1937 sales exceeded 11,000 for the first time since 1930. The same year brought significant improvements elsewhere in the range: full roller bearing engines, chromolly (chrome-molybdenum steel) fork tubes, and interchangeable wheels.

As well as these technical advances, the lessons of the Depression had instilled in the company a belief in the importance of styling and cosmetic attraction – for many the essence of Harleys today. The aftermarket and art deco

Above: When launched in 1936 the Knucklehead was the first of a new breed of overhead-valve Harleys. Early examples were all of 61cu.in (989cc). Pictured is a 1946 74cu.in (1207cc) example.

innovations of 1932 were continued. Balloon tyres appeared in 1940 (more striking, if less functional, than new aluminium alloy heads for the 'flathead' side-valve models). In 1941, four-speed transmissions became standard across the over-45-inch range. Eleven models were now on the books in four basic engine configurations: side-valves of 45, 74 and 80 cubic inches; and Knuckleheads of 61 and 74 cubic inches.

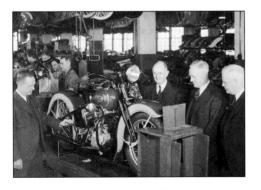

Above: H-D's founders inspect the first Knucklehead off the line in 1936.

By 1941 production had risen from a low of 3703 in 1933, to over 18,000 in 1941 (excluding military sales). Harley had made it. They had been through the hell of the Thirties and come out stronger than ever before. What they perhaps didn't appreciate was just how well the new image would equip them for a motorcycle market still half a century in the future.

Left and Below: The same '46 FL pictured on a Californian beach. In hot climates many owners preferred its better cooled – but leakier – lubrication system to the later Panhead's.

FL Knucklehead

THE Knuckle is many motorcyclists' idea of the quintessential Harley. Formally designated the Model E, in making its debut in 1936 it announced – as far as any piece of hardware is capable of speech – 'The Depression is over.'

As usual the Knuckle was initially available in three guises: E (standard), ES (sidecar) and EL (high compression sport). And Joe Petrali's influence was clear. With 40 horsepower at 4800rpm, the EL, in particular, offered a huge performance increase over the laggard side-valvers. Yet despite its leisurely route to production, and not for the first time, there were initial problems.

The worst of these concerned its dry-sump lubrication. Some parts got too little oil; others – including the road underneath – got too much. 1937 brought a partial fix, but the glitch was not licked fully until the arrival of a centrifugally-controlled oil pump by-pass with the 74cu in (1200cc) Model F Knuckle in 1941. Although notorious for oil leaks through its many external seals, and with separate primary drive oiling, in very hot conditions many riders preferred the big Knuckle's oil system to that of the later 'improved' Panhead.

Although Harley comfortably outsold their rival Indian in the US market overall, the 74-inch Knucklehead came about largely in response to competition from large capacity Indian V-twins. The bigger engine's extra torque demanded a new seven-plate clutch in place of the old five-plate device. In addition there was a bigger rear brake

(American's have always been oddly suspicious of front stoppers, yet 565lb (256kg) of iron takes some slowing), a larger air-cleaner (essential in the dusty West) and 'airplane-style' speedometer.

Despite its hallowed reputation, the Knuckle never quite made the impact it deserved. But for the Depression, it would certainly have reached production earlier. Then, no sooner had the 74-inch version eased the high spots off its bores, than the Japanese attacked Pearl Harbor in December 1941, and the factory was quickly diverted to military production. Milwaukee lore has it that the very best of the big Knuckles were those built in that final pre-war year, but hostilities meant that relatively few 74-inch Knuckles reached the road until 1947. And by 1948, the Knuckle was history.

SPECIFICATION	MODEL E 'KNUCKLEHEAD'
ENGINE	61cu.in (988cc) ohv V-twin (also later 74cu.in version)
POWER	40bhp @ 4800rpm
TRANSMISSION	4-speed
WHEELBASE	59.5in (1511mm)
FUEL TANK	3.2 gallons (14.6 litres)
WEIGHT (dry)	565lb (256kg)
TOP SPEED	around 90mph (145km/h)

All pictures: Almost any modern Harley fan would yearn to own a machine such as this – although actually riding it might be a different matter. The combination of hand gear change and foot clutch makes controlled take-offs a far from easy matter.

Back To War

AS AMERICA'S largest motorcycle producer, it fell to Harley-Davidson to underpin the bulk of the country's two-wheeled war effort. Throughout the war years, the entire output of the Milwaukee factory was turned over to military production.

Planning for anticipated military needs had begun in the autumn of 1939, shortly after the outbreak of war in Europe, but two years before

Below: Perhaps Harley should have avoided another flat twin after the failure of the earlier Model W. The shaft-drive XA was produced only in small numbers for military use.

America would directly enter the fray. Early work, in competition with Indian and Delco, focussed on an army requirement for a three-wheeler for rough terrain. The project never reached fruition, but ironically Harley did win a contract to supply 1000 machines with an engine similar to that envisaged by Delco's contender. Other projects were more bizarre still, including an armoured machine-gun carrier and a prototype powerplant for a small tank comprising two linked 61-inch (1000cc) overhead-valve engines.

The one that did reach production was the Model XA, powered by a horizontally-opposed flathead twin displacing 45cu in (743cc). With shaft final drive and plunger rear suspension, it was specifically designed for use in the North African desert. The XA's engine and transmission was

similar in appearance to the German Zündapp or BMW, with which it has sometimes been confused in contemporary photographs. A more secret mission was the stripping and assessment of a Russian motorcycle for US intelligence, a task we can be grateful did not lead to the production of Dnepr replicas at Juneau Avenue.

Nor was Harley's wartime contribution confined to hardware. John E. Harley, later in charge of the parts and accessories division, rose to the rank of major in the Second World War. Among his tasks, and one to which he was ideally suited, was the training of army motorcyclists at Fort Knox, Kentucky.

But by far the bulk of Harley-Davidson's war effort was geared to the production of military versions of the WL V-twin, designated WLA, for Army. Of almost 90,000 Harleys 'enlisted', around 88,000 were good ol' 45-inch (743cc) WLAs. The same attributes of rugged simplicity which had conferred on the side-valve twin such a dependable peacetime reputation made it ideally suited to the harsher demands of war.

As with the First World War, the Second was fairly good to Milwaukee. In 1940, sales had totalled less than 11,000. These soared to 18,000 as the military build-up began in 1941, reaching over 29,000 in each of the following two years, before tailing off again as peace approached. But Harley iron was good to America, too – a fact recognized by the award of two coveted Army-Navy 'E' awards for excellence in wartime production. Milwaukee's factory workers couldn't necessarily go to war with the enemy, but they could sure as hell help those guys who did.

Right and below: What did you do in the war, daddy? These WLA model GIs aren't telling, but the twin served proudly during the Second World War with British as well as American forces.

O-LCT 88 IN
O-HGT 41.
O-WTH 36.

RAF

Post-War: The Panhead Years

WHEN THE war ended, what everyone wanted was wheels, and more modern wheels at that. In 1945 Harley resumed civilian motorcycle production, although (partly due to industrial action) it would be 1947 before sales regained their pre-war level. A year later still, the much-anticipated replacement for the noble Knucklehead made its first public appearance.

The Panhead as it became known, was a development of the Knuckle rather than an all-new concept. As well as a revised (and much more oil-tight) lubrication system, the Pan featured aluminium alloy cylinder heads in place of the Knuckle's iron, and hydraulic tappets (or 'lifters', as Americans prefer), rather than 'solid' push-rods. So named because its rocker covers resembled inverted baking pans, the Pan was built in both 74cu in (1208cc) and 61cu in (988cc) sizes, although the latter was discontinued in '53. The larger version retained the 'traditional' bore and stroke dimensions of 87 by 102mm (or rather, as Americans still prefer it, 3⁷/₁₆ by 4 inches).

At least as enduring was the name given to the 1949 model which bore this engine. The Hydra-Glide of 1949 was the first Harley to employ hydraulically-damped telescopic front forks. It was also, of course, the first model granted one of the most evocative titles in motorcycling: 'Glide'. The Panhead engine would do much to get the species on its famous way, propelling not only the Duo-Glide of 1958, but the first of the Electra Glides, as well.

But the Hydra- was more than merely the first Glide. They didn't know it at the time, but this was the model that was to set the visual cues for the 'retro-tech' Harleys which would appear four decades later. From its deeply-valanced mudguards

Left and above: The Panhead – named for its pan-shaped valve covers – replaced the Knuckle in 1948, although their bottom-ends were much the same.

Left: In addition to the new Panhead engine, the Hydra Glide was the first Harley model with telescopic front suspension. Perhaps more important, it was the first model designated 'glide'.

SPECIFICATION	HYDRA-GLIDE
ENGINE	74cu.in (1207cc) ohv V-twin (also 61cu.in version)
POWER	50bhp @ 4800rpm (55bhp from 1951)
TRANSMISSION	4-speed
WHEELBASE	59.5in (1511mm)
FUEL TANK	3.2 gallons (14.6 litres)
WEIGHT (dry)	560lb (254kg)
TOP SPEED	around 95mph (153km/h)

to its stylized rear end, the style of the modern Softail owes much to the Hydra-Glide.

1947 was also the year in which Harley-Davidson unveiled a second factory plant on Capitol Drive, Wauwatosa. Within a year, production was at an all-time high. Less auspiciously for V-twin die-hards, November '47 marked the debut of the 1.7 horsepower Model S 125cc two-stroke single. This was based on the same German DKW RT125 design as the BSA Bantam (and later Yamaha's very first model, the YA1 'Red Dragonfly') – and was marketed on the mistaken presumption that demobbed GIs would buy almost anything with wheels. In '53 the engine grew to 165cc, powering the Model ST, then, for five years from 1960, the ill-conceived Topper scooter. Perhaps the best-known version, the 125cc Model B Hummer, produced 3bhp and ran from 1955-59.

OLD NAMES, NEW FACES

When Arthur Davidson died in a car accident on 30 December 1950, the last of the original founders had gone. William A. had died in 1937, Walter in 1942 and Bill Harley one year later. The company nonetheless remained in solid Harley-Davidson hands – and again the latter family outnumbered the former three-to-one. William H. Davidson had joined the company in 1928, became president in 1942 and would hold that position until the Seventies. The other sons employed in the family business were Gordon and Walter C. Davidson and William J. Harley.

The Eagle And The Bulldog

THINK OF Harley, and you think of style – right? But it wasn't always so. In the Fifties, Triumph had the image: Marlon Brando's. When the young rebel cut loose on a Triumph Thunderbird in *The Wild One* in 1952, it was heaven-sent publicity material. In a single cinematic swoop, Triumph had become part of US youth culture.

Although Harley-Davidson was to lose one competitor with the demise of Indian in 1953, it frightened them half to death when Triumph set up their US import network in 1951. Isolated by war, supported by military production, Harley had had it too easy for too long. Triumph had a much broader range of cheaper, yet much more exciting and

technically sophisticated models than Harley (whose flagship FL model persisted with hand-change until 1952), and a vibrant young organization to back them up.

Milwaukee's response was to bully its dealers into having no business with the British upstart. Then, in 1952, Harley applied for government protection. They wanted not only a 40 per cent

Below: A gleaming 1958 Duo Glide pictured in Harley-Davidson's superb museum at York, Pennsylvania, USA.

import tax, but also quotas on the number of machines that Triumph (and parent company BSA) could import. (On America's dirt racetracks, they employed the now familiar ploy of handicapping the opposition. In this case, foreign ohv engines, competing against 750cc Harley flatheads, were limited to 500cc.)

Thirty years later, thanks to President Reagan, Harley got the protection it wanted, this time from the Japanese. But first time around, they didn't: after two weeks of hearings the Tariff Commission decided that Triumph had no case to answer. Then they put Harley in the dock and told them to quit their restrictive trading practices!

It's only a small exaggeration to suggest that Triumph, BSA – and to a lesser extent Norton and Royal Enfield – invented the modern US market (although it was only fully to explode into life with the arrival of the Japanese 15 years later). The sales figures show the full extent of the problem. In 1948, Harley-Davidson produced over 31,000 machines (a figure they would not exceed again until 1966). Then sales plummeted to a low of 9,750 in 1955.

A measure of Harley's problem was the Model

SPECIFICATION	MODEL K
ENGINE	45cu.in (750cc) side-valve V-twin (also 55cu.in version)
POWER	30bhp @ 4500rpm
TRANSMISSION	4-speed
WHEELBASE	N/A
FUEL TANK	3.6 gallons (16.4 litres)
TOP SPEED	around 80mph (129km/h)

K, introduced in 1952. Whilst British twins offered overhead valves, lightweight construction, good suspension at both ends (and, in the case of Norton, the finest handling available anywhere, at almost any price), the K proffered a massively heavy 45cu in (750cc) sidevalve design. True, there was now proper suspension at both ends – a first for Milwaukee – but it was woefully outclassed.

Harley claimed 30 horsepower for the Model K, only a little less than the contemporary Triumph Thunderbird. Whether true or not, the 85mph (137km/h) – on a good day – V-twin was no match

Above: The Model K's lasting gift to posterity was the unit-construction Sportster which superseded it in 1957. This is a 1959 XLH high-compression version.

for the 103mph (166km/h) Britisher. The KHK version, with hotter cams, was better. There were also serious early mechanical problems, although quality, and power, improved somewhat with a capacity increase to 55cu in (883cc) in 1954. Remarkably, in 1954, Joe Leonard became first US national champion on a machine substantially derived from the K.

If the original Model K was no world-beater, the machine which superseded it in 1957 has certainly stood the test of time. But the XL Sportster was a much finer machine in every respect. Although now displacing an actual 53.9cu in (883cc, as today), the XL had much more. The engine and gearbox were now in-unit (an improvement that Harley, for once, beat their major opposition to). There was a full swing-arm rear suspension with car-type shock absorbers, allowing early Sportsters to be sold as suitable for either on- or off-road use. It was an instant hit, accounting for almost 20 per cent of Harley's 1957 production of over 13,000 machines.

Below: Remarkably, this is a '58 Duo Glide, too, although it has more in common with Dennis Hopper's chopped mount in the film Easy Rider *than with the standard model seen on page 28. Although substantially the same as the Hydra Glide, when introduced in 1958 the Duo was Harley's first deluxe model with front and rear suspension. By this time, however, the opposition had moved ahead.*

SCOOTIN' WITH HARLEY-D

If Harley-Davidson and BSA were deadly rivals throughout this period, they did have one thing in common: both made misguided assaults on the emerging scooter market.

Where the BSA group's scoot was the Triumph Tigress, Harley's version was named the Topper. Launched in 1960 and powered by the same 165cc two-stroke engine as the old ST, it was offered in both five and nine horsepower versions to suit local state laws. Like most scooters, it boasted many clever design touches, and some downright weird ones (it was started with a rope like an outboard motor, and for some reason was deemed to need a parking brake). Like its British counterparts, the Topper missed out on the scooter boom and quietly – mercifully – subsided in 1965.

In 1958 the good got better, thanks to lighter valvegear, higher compression and gas-flowed heads. Another year and one of the most legendary Harleys ever appeared, the XLCH – 'Competition Hot'. The Sportster also looked the part – cut down, lean and purposeful, with its tiny tank and raucous 'shorty' exhausts. Improvements followed year on year: electric start (1967), progressively more power (58bhp in 1968), and larger displacements – first 61cu in (988cc) (1972), then Evolution-engined versions of 55cu in (883cc) and 67cu in (1100cc) (1986), and ultimately 74cu in (1200cc). Along the way there were striking variations like the low-riding Hugger (1979) and the seminal, limited-edition XR1000 of 1983. And, not least, the Sportster is father to the remarkable XR750 racer which continues to dominate America's dirt tracks.

Nor was development attention denied to Milwaukee's heavyweights. As the Fifties drew to a close the Hydra-Glide finally got the rear suspension it deserved, and the Model F Duo-Glide was born. As well as a swinging-fork rear end, the Duo featured the novelty of a hydraulic rear brake – something of a gimmick, since both hubs contained tiny six-inch (152mm) drums which struggled to haul down the Glide's substantial bulk. But an unlikely bonus was around the corner: Dennis Hopper would ride one (albeit much chopped) in the cult movie *Easy Rider*.

Below: They didn't call it 'Topper' because it was comic but they might have. The scooter was another ill-fated post-war venture.

SPECIFICATION	XL SPORTSTER
ENGINE	53.9cu.in (883cc) ohv V-twin (later versions 61 and 67cu.in)
POWER	40bhp @ 5500rpm (1957)
TRANSMISSION	4-speed
WHEELBASE	60in (1524mm)
FUEL TANK	3.5 gallons (16.0 litres)
WEIGHT (dry)	454lb (205kg)
TOP SPEED	around 96mph (155km/h)

The Italian Connection

DESPITE the success of the Sportster and consistent, if modest, profits, by the late Fifties Harley-Davidson's sales decline was entrenched. The western world was witnessing a major boom in motorcycle sales, and Milwaukee naturally wanted a part of it.

Much of this boom centred around sales of lightweight machines. Harley had tried this route with the 165cc ST, and would try again with the 125cc Hummer and latterly the Topper scooter. But it was becoming clear to the men of the Development Committee, charged with planning the company's future, that the best route to a more diverse model range might be collaboration with an overseas company.

Eventually a deal was struck in which Harley bought half of the motorcycle division of the Italian company Aeronautica Macchi SpA (the parent company also made aircraft), for the bargain price of just under $250,000. Harley were anticipating the joint venture to generate some 6000 lightweight sales per year, to be produced in Varese.

Although two-strokes would later bring Harley-Aermacchi more racing success, the Italian flat singles were true classics both on road and track. Left is a 1967 works 350cc bike.

The first Harley-Aermacchi, the 250 Sprint, arrived in September 1960. This was based upon a horizontal, single-cylinder, four-stroke design similar to that of the famous Aermacchi racers, although most subsequent 'joint venture' models would be small two-strokes. It was light, fast (25 horsepower by 1964), handled well and produced a superb line of racing machines. Yet it, and its stablemates, all failed to live up to Harley's commercial expectations – much as had Indian's dabbling in middleweights, three decades before.

The reasons were many. Communications between Milwaukee and Varese were attenuated, at best. There were continuous supply problems with bought-in components, and in their compatibility with US parts. When AMF took over Harley in 1968 (see page 36), specifications were often changed erratically, without appropriate consultation or re-pricing. But most of all, the products weren't wanted: they weren't wanted either by a public being offered Japanese machines of ever-more exotic specification at lower prices; and now they weren't much wanted by dealers who had to re-learn their business, carry new parts stock, and all for a much smaller profit margin per machine.

There were high-points, of course – not least Walter Villa's consecutive world 250cc road race titles in 1974 and '75 – but with *two-strokes*? But on the whole it was an unrewarding marriage, and divorce came far too late. Eventually, in June 1978,

SPECIFICATION	AERMACCHI 350 RACER
ENGINE	344cc ohv horizontal single
POWER	38bhp @ 8500rpm
COMPRESSION	11.4:1
TRANSMISSION	5-speed
WHEELBASE	53in (1346mm)
FUEL TANK	2.9 gallons (13 litres)
WEIGHT (dry)	245lb (111kg)
TOP SPEED	around 130mph (209km/h)

Harley closed their Italian factory. Four years later it began producing a new machine with an unusual name, Cagiva, which was later to embrace legendary V-twins of its own.

33

1965 FL Panhead Electra Glide

NO OTHER name in motorcycling strikes quite the same chord in the ears of the public at large as Harley's long-time flagship cruiser. The Electra Glide was a development of the '58 Duo-Glide, itself essentially a Hydra-Glide with rear suspension. The first Electra Glide was also the last of the Panheads, since from 1966 the Shovelhead engine took over the Electra Glide mantle until the last of the breed was built in June 1984.

The Electra Glide was so-named for its novel electric starter, and there was a new five-gallon (US) (18.2lit) 'turnpike' tank. But in other respects it was little changed from the Duo-Glide. The Panhead engine had received major revisions in 1955, before it reverted in 1964 to the Knucklehead's external top end oil feeds in an attempt to prevent overheating. The conversion to electric start also required an upgrade to 12 volt electrics and a huge 32Ah battery. The starter motor itself lived behind the rear cylinder and engaged on the rear of the primary drive. Surprisingly for a unit 'borrowed' from an outboard motor, the first starters were troublesome if the weather was damp, and the kick start was prudently retained. Harley later adopted Homelite starters, which were much more reliable.

Like all Harley vees, the ohv engine ran forked con-rods to eliminate rocking couple. Primary drive was by chain to a four-speed box (with a sidecar option, up to 1980, of three forward and one reverse). Capacity was 74cu in (1208cc): the current 80-inch (1340cc) dimensions didn't arrive until 1970

and the new generation of 'alternator' Shovelheads. Harley claimed 55 horsepower for the hottest Pan, with the 'power pac' FLH Shovel producing 5bhp more.

From a rider's point of view, this motorcycle is not a device for rustling through the ratios, which swap with mule-like eagerness. It's a laid-back tourer – a device for getting into top, and staying there as you head for the next horizon. The steering is equally ponderous, the ground clearance poor and

the single leading-shoe front brake laughably ineffective. But like most Harleys, the rear brake, with something like 700lb (317kg) tying it to the floor, is surprisingly good.

But handsome it certainly is, with its whitewall tyres, gleaming chrome and low-slung looks. A 'King of the Road' touring pack offered in 1966 required the relocation forward of the rear shock absorbers, further to the detriment of the Glide's already abysmal handling. But, boy, was it cool.

All pictures: One of the best-looking Harleys of all time, this exquisite machine is the first of the Electra Glides, a '65 Panhead. Many of its elements can be seen on the latest Milwaukee iron, not least the chromed badge on the deeply-valanced mudguards. After 1965 the Panhead gave way to the slightly more powerful Shovelhead engine with 'power pac' heads, although the two engines shared similar crankcases. The Shovel was also held to vibrate and leak oil less than the Pan. According to its owner, a former missile engineer, the front 'stopper' is little more than a parking brake.

SPECIFICATION	1965 PANHEAD ELECTRA GLIDE
ENGINE	74cu.in (1207cc) ohv V-twin
POWER	50bhp @ 4800rpm
TRANSMISSION	4-speed
WHEELBASE	61in (1550mm)
FUEL TANK	4.0 gallons (18.2 litres)
WEIGHT (dry)	555lb (252kg)
TOP SPEED	around 96mph (155km/h)

35

Goodbye Milwaukee, Hello AMF

IN HARLEY lore, 1965 is best remembered for two enduring events. The first was the unveiling of a new generation of Shovelhead engines, replacing the venerable Panheads. Second, and ultimately far more momentous, was the decision to list the company on the stock-market – in other words, to lose complete control.

During the next four years over 1.3 million Harley shares were sold, pleasing investors, for the company's performance was good. But less happy times were approaching, as a rising tide of new models began to rush in from Japan. Initially these were middleweights – light, fast and refined machines – but soon Honda would begin a full-frontal heavyweight assault with the awesome, four-cylinder CB750.

At the same time, Harley came under threat of takeover from an industrial conglomerate including the Waukesha Engine Company which was busily accumulating H-D stock. Alarmed, in 1968 company president William H. Davidson resumed previous talks with American Machine and Foundry

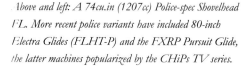

Above and left: A 74cu.in (1207cc) Police-spec Shovelhead FL. More recent police variants have included 80-inch Electra Glides (FLHT-P) and the FXRP Pursuit Glide, the latter machines popularized by the CHiPs TV series.

(AMF), another industrial giant with sights on Harley, but with a far less predatory reputation. A bidding war followed, during which Harley recommended AMF's offer to its shareholders, most of whom did very well out of the subsequent deal. On 18th December 1968, Milwaukee's finest became AMF property.

But if there was a honeymoon period under the new management, it was short. Over the next few years, a succession of Harley's best men left. And although William H. Davidson was named chairman in 1971, it was a toothless appointment as he retained little say in the production and design of motorcycles.

SHOVELHEAD: 1966-84

First seen on the '66 Electra Glide, the Shovelhead engine followed the usual Harley practice of bolting a new top-end onto the previous tried-and-tested crankcases. A new bottom-end finally arrived in 1970, in which a crankshaft-mounted alternator replaced the previous generator (and made the engine even wider). These are easily recognized by their cone-shaped right-side engine covers. Originally produced in 74-inch (1200cc) form, Shovels grew to 80cu in (1340cc) in 1978, when electronic ignition was also added.

SPECIFICATION	SHOVELHEAD FL
ENGINE	74cu.in (1207cc) ohv V-twin
POWER	60bhp @ 5400rpm
TORQUE	62lb.ft @ 3200rpm
TRANSMISSION	4-speed
WHEELBASE	60in (1524mm)
FUEL TANK	4gallons (18.2 litres)
WEIGHT (dry)	around 600lb (272kg)
TOP SPEED	around 103mph (164km/h)

These events tend to overshadow the hardware produced during the AMF years. The popular opinion now is that AMF starved and milked the company, that it didn't understand motorcycles, that quality went to the dogs and that Harley/AMF never built a decent bike. While some of this is undoubtedly true, it is undeniable that AMF sank millions of dollars into their new baby. During the first three years of their tenure total sales (including Italian machines) more than doubled; and during their 12 years in control sales of US-made machines more than tripled. Additionally, there was diversification into such unlikely fields as snowmobiles and desert racers. But if sales were reasonably strong, profits were not, and AMF grew increasingly disenchanted with the motorcycle business (even though AMF chairman Rodney C. Gott was a keen motorcyclist). Difficult labour relations at strongly unionized Harley were a significant part of this concern.

There were long-term effects. One was the 1972 departure of Harley's assembly operations from their Milwaukee 'shrine' to a vacant AMF plant in York, Pennsylvania (where it remains to this day, although Milwaukee has always made engines). Another was the startling styling innovations created by William ('Willie') G. Davidson, initially with the 1971 Super Glide. Then there was AMF's marketing and promotion expertise, which certainly rubbed off onto the future independent Harley company. Indeed, both are at the heart of the company's ethos today – but there would by trying times before they could fully take effect.

Below: This '70s Shovelhead is a police model. Poor quality during the AMF years lost Harley many police contracts.

Challenge From The East

NOSTALGIA tells us that the Seventies had produced some classic Harley models, such as the 1971 Super Glide, and the XLCR Cafe Racer and Low Rider in '77. Even the Eighties arrived promisingly enough, with the five-speed, rubber-mounted Tour Glide, the Wide Glide and the belt-drive FXB Sturgis. Yet at the start of the 1980s few people gave AMF Harley-Davidson much chance of survival.

Whatever AMF's shortcomings, Harley's biggest problem during their years in control lay in a quite different direction. After all, it was scarcely AMF's fault that this period happened to coincide so precisely with the rise of the Japanese motorcycle industry to global domination.

Yet it's also a myth that Japan stole the American motorcycle market, either from Harley-Davidson or from the Europeans. In the mid Fifties annual US sales of new models stood at around the 60,000 mark. By 1973 they had peaked at no less than 1.5 million motorcycles sold. This staggering increase was almost solely due to the inventiveness and enterprise of the Japanese, who produced reliable, fast and exciting machines light years more advanced than any Harley, at a far lower price. And,

Right: One of the raunchiest Harleys ever built, the all-black XLCR 'Café racer' dates from 1972. Below: A striking 1973 Sportster special, dubbed XR900 and intended to imitate the lines of Milwaukee's XR750 flat-track racers.

whatever 'image' Harleys might with hindsight possess, few buyers were prepared to pay the price for it at the time. Much the same, of course, was true of British motorcycles.

This didn't stop Harley-Davidson from alleging that Oriental success was in part due to cut-price 'dumping' of Japanese models. Formal complaint was made to the US government. Eventually the trade commission agreed that dumping had taken place, but that the effective subsidy was minute. More embarrassingly still, it concluded that the practice had not significantly harmed Harley sales, but rather that Harley's obsolete models were the prime cause of their decline.

But for Harley the situation was desperate, the more so because AMF had to some extent

attempted to compete head-on with Japan, rather than concentrating on the more specialized market that Harley suited. Production figures for 1982 offer some measure of the hopelessness of such a strategy: Honda built over 3.5 million bikes in the year; Harley built just over 30,000.

The nett effect was that Harley's share of the rapidly growing US big-bike market plunged from almost 100 per cent in 1973 to less than 40 per cent by late 1979. Worse still was the high price, low profits and poor build quality of Harleys, who (like countless other US companies) simply could not manufacture their product half as well as the Japanese.

In late 1975, AMF put Vaughn Beals in charge of Harley. He and chief engineer Jeff Bleustein struggled to alert top managers to the production realities they had to face. Beals set up a quality control and inspection programme that began to eliminate the worst of the problems, but at a prodigious cost: on early examples of one new model, it had cost about $1000 extra to make each bike fit for sale at around $4000. Nonetheless, Beals' efforts slowly began to put Harley back on track. But what they really needed was a new engine. And by 1980, with AMF losing interest, the scene was set for change.

What Harleys do best: a Tour Glide cruising on the banks of the Mississippi at sunset on a long, hot summer's day. They might not corner too well, but all Glides have a knack of devouring miles effortlessly to the easy thump of the 1340cc Evo engine.

39

Style King: FX Super Glide

THE 1971 Super Glide was the first major new twin launched by Harley after the takeover by AMF, and for all the new owner's staid reputation it was the most exciting new model in years. Conceived and styled by Willie G. Davidson, the grandson of one of H-D's founders, this was to set Harley down a road of factory customs which continues with undiminished brilliance to this day. Indeed, this was the very first factory custom. Previously, any rider wanting something this different had to build it himself.

The new Glide was essentially a union of F-series Shovelhead engine and frame, with an X-series (Sportster) front end. At the rear, a 'boat-tail' Sportster seat completed a graphic ensemble quite unlike anything Harley – or anyone else – had produced before. It looked great and went well – a 70lb (32kg) weight reduction compared to a stock FL saw to that.

Below: Willie G's first masterpiece, the original Super Glide of 1971, was essentially a Sportster front end grafted onto an F-series engine and chassis. This FXE 1200 version dates from 1979, by which time the earlier 'boat-tail' rear end had disappeared.

Right: By 1974 this electric-start version of the FX 1200, the FXE, was on sale, now also with disc front brake in place of the '71 model's ludicrously feeble single leading shoe drum. From the success of the Super Glide, Willie G's fertile imagination spawned countless eye-catching variants.

Despite the splash it made at the time – most road tests raved about the new custom machine – early examples were decidedly under-specified. Disc brakes finally arrived in 1973, and an electric start option (the FXE) in 1974. Eight years later an even more innovative descendant , the FXR and FXRS 'Super Glide II', would feature five-speed gearboxes and new frames with rubber-mounted engines, leading to the half-faired FXRT Sport Glide of '86.

1977 brought another classic derivative from Willie G.'s fertile imagination, the FXS Low Rider, complete with standard highway pegs, Fat Bob two-piece petrol tank and a seat just 27 inches (686mm) above the ground.

The Super Glide's pick'n'mix philosophy – one bit from this model, some from another and more parts from a third – became the essence of all the most memorable Harleys since. The range of available options increased with the introduction of the 80cu in (1340cc) Shovelhead engine, initially on the Electra Glide, in 1978. This led one year later to the FLH-80, offered as standard with a complete set of touring extras which was later to become the long-haul norm: saddlebags, luggage rack, fairing, running boards and additional lights. This in turn led to the FLT Tour Glide of 1980, similar to the full-dress Glide but with better brakes and a larger, twin-headlamp touring fairing. More significantly still, the FLT featured Harley's first five-speed

transmission and, not least, the first rubber-mounted engine.

Nor was the rest of the range neglected in the vintage year of 1980. The Super Glide became the FXB Sturgis, named after the famous Hog rally held annually in South Dakota. The 'B' represented the first toothed rubber belt drive – a clean and trouble-free system now standard across the range. For good measure there was the FXWG Wide Glide and FXEF Fat Bob.

SPECIFICATION	FX SUPER GLIDE
ENGINE	74cu.in (1207cc) ohv V-twin
POWER	60bhp @ 5400rpm
TORQUE	65lb.ft @ 3200rpm
TRANSMISSION	4-speed
WHEELBASE	60in (1524mm)
FUEL TANK	3.0 gallons (13.7 litres)
WEIGHT (dry)	528lb (240kg)
TOP SPEED	around 105mph (169km/h)

41

The Eagle Soars Alone

IN 1981, the AMF chapter in the Harley-Davidson story drew to a close in what was probably the most momentous – and certainly the most audacious – episode in the company's long history. Early in 1981, chairman Vaughn Beals persuaded 12 other Harley executives to join him in taking over the company in an $81.5 million leveraged buyout from AMF control. The group found a willing lead lender in Citicorp, and after several months of tough bargaining with AMF, the independent Harley-Davidson Motor Co. began business on 16 June 1981.

The event, not surprisingly, was accompanied by much fanfare of the 'The Eagle Soars Alone' variety, including a symbolic ride out by the new owners from Milwaukee to York. Now Harley was owned and run by real motorcyclists, men who loved the big V-twins, men who really cared. They were heady days, but on its own the euphoria counted for nothing because the American market, and even more so Harley's portion of it, was about to cave in. Far from the buy-out enhancing their fortunes, by 1983 Harley's share of the now-shrinking USA big-bike pot had declined even further to a mere 23 per cent.

The truth was that whoever ran Harley had to understand one fundamental truth: the Japanese were still producing better bikes at lower cost. How did they do it? Beals and other managers had toured Japanese plants in 1980, but it wasn't until after the buyout when they got the opportunity to inspect the Honda assembly plant in Marysville, Ohio, that they began to understand. Chairman Vaughn Beals remarked that 'We found it hard to believe we could be that bad – but we were. We were being wiped out by the Japanese because they were better managers. It wasn't robotics, or culture, or morning callisthenics and company songs – it was professional managers who understood their business and paid attention to detail.'

The message wasn't lost on the new team. Within less than four months, with help from industrial consultants Andersen Consulting, a pilot programme of 'just-in-time' and other novel (for Harley) production systems began. When that showed promise, Tom Gelb, in charge of production, told his employees that, 'We have to play the game the way the Japanese play it or we're dead.'

The other arm of the new strategy came as Harley shifted its marketing focus, stopped trying to compete against the Japanese, and threw all of its resources into developing what we now take for granted as its uniquely American big-bike niche.

But the question wasn't so much 'Could they make the necessary changes?', as 'Could they survive long enough to try?' After losing $25 million in 1982, it looked doubtful. These were perilous times.

Below: Reflection in chrome: Manhattan Beach custom shop.

Thank You, Mr President

Below: Harley Owners Group and other activities encourage V-twin owners as part of a whole lifestyle package. The scheme has since been imitated by other manufacturers.

WHAT Harley desperately needed after the management buyout was a little breathing space. Some of it came from an unlikely source.

In August 1982 another Harley delegation made the trip to Washington, again alleging illegal trading practices by the rival Japanese motorcycle companies. The Trade Commission was again told that cheap motorcycles were being dumped on the market, and further that the Japanese were 'virtually copying' Harley models, all of which was seriously undermining their sales. On All Fools Day 1983 the White House announced that President Reagan had found in Harley's favour and would impose tariffs on Japanese machines.

The tariffs would apply to all imported models of over 700cc, initially at the hefty rate of 45 per cent (in addition to the existing 4.4 per cent duty), decreasing year-by-year until 1988. Although some Japanese manufacturers were able to sidestep the new measures on machines built in the US, such as Honda Gold Wings, the levy was inevitably a major factor in helping Harley-Davidson's regeneration. In the meantime they had to continue to improve quality and efficiency and – most crucially of all – come up with a replacement for the aged Shovelhead.

Not the least of the hurdles was convincing potential buyers that Harley had truly solved its notorious AMF quality problems. To bring home the message, in 1984 the company spent $3 million on an unprecedented 'Super Ride' demonstration

program. A series of TV commercials invited bikers to visit any of the 600-plus dealers to road test a new Harley. Over three weekends, the company gave 90,000 rides to 40,000 people, half of whom owned other brands. The venture didn't sell enough bikes to cover its cost, but it did make a point: hey, guys, maybe these things really have changed.

But nothing set the tone for new Harley quite as emphatically as the Harley Owners' Group (HOG) programme, a factory-sponsored club which sought to bring customers together in the H-D lifestyle in a way which had never been attempted before. A soaraway success, HOG now

boasts well over 100,000 committed members in the USA alone, and has become the envy of every other motorcycle manufacturer.

Slowly, Vaughn Beals and his team began to turn it all around. After a crushing deficit in 1982, the company edged back into the black in 1983 and made a profit of $2.9 million on sales of $294 million in 1984. It was steadily catching mighty Honda in the heavyweight market, improving quality and production efficiency, marketing more aggressively, and beginning to make the most of its uniquely American image. There was still a long way to go, but it was a helluva start.

43

Revolution And Rebirth

THE YEAR 1984 was a distinctly mixed bag at Harley. The good news was the much anticipated arrival of a new replacement for the Shovelhead. This, the 80cu in (1340cc) Evolution engine, looked like the answer, particularly when later reinforced by a 55-inch (883cc) stablemate. Retro-tech had also arrived with the '84 Softail – the only model to boast the new Evo motor in that first year – and would shortly be followed by the '85 Heritage Softail, allied to new Sportster and 'Super Glide II' models previously launched in '82. The 883 Sportster, in particular, with an initial price of just under $4000, was the type of entry-level machine so conspicuously lacking in the past. Suddenly Harley had a credible range, a growing reputation for reliability, and for the first time in a decade had a product capable of meeting police specifications.

Yet financial gremlins continued to gnaw at the company's foundations. Citicorp Bank, which had financed the management buyout, was concerned about Harley's future once the tariff on foreign competitors was lifted in 1988. The bank reasoned that it had the best chance of getting a

Below: H-D revolutionized both manufacturing and style.

Right: The 'Entry-level' Harley-Davidson is this surprisingly affordable 883cc XL Sportster model, now available with five-speed transmission and toothed belt final drive.

good price for the company and recovering its money while sales were still on the rise. In order not to further increase its risk, in November 1984 the bank shocked Harley with the news that its credit would be severely restricted from the following year. This was a major blow not only to Harley's future plans, but to the survival of the buyout venture, for the company was effectively broke.

Over the summer of 1985, Vaughn Beals and chief financial officer Richard Teerlink (later to succeed Beals as Harley's head), chased vainly after new lenders – 'hawking begging bowls around Wall Street', as memorably described at the time. Then, at the eleventh hour and with the lawyers already drafting bankruptcy plans, Beals and Teerlink were put in touch with the Heller Financial Corporation. Luckily for Beals, Heller's No. 2, Bob Koe, was a long-time Harley buff and more than ready to listen. He was impressed by what he heard, and a financial package was agreed on 23 December 1985 – the best Christmas present Harley could wish. The new lenders would pay Citicorp $49 million ($8 million less than it had poured in, although it would later recover $6 million in credits) and supply Harley with $49.5 million in working capital.

It turned out to be a good deal for everyone but Citicorp, who had badly underestimated the vibrant new Harley's outlook. Sales for 1985 gave Harley 28 per cent of the big bike market. Then, with supreme irony, within a year of being abandoned by Citicorp, Harley would recover the

over-850cc No. 1 spot from Honda with 33 per cent. The long struggle to improve production and marketing standards and regenerate the model range was finally beginning to pay dividends. Profits for 1986 were a healthy $4.3 million on sales of $295 million.

H-D's financial base was eventually secured in July '87 when their shares were approved for listing on the New York Stock Exchange, a far better deal for their enthusiasts than Norton's similar venture in Britain, for the shares have since tripled in value. The offer raised over £30 million, allowing the company to reschedule its debts and buy the Holiday Rambler Corporation, a leading manufacturer of recreational vehicles. Less comforting, although it made sound financial sense,

was the closure of the competition department, although production of XR750 dirt-track engines was unaffected, and racing continued in the famous black and orange livery through the involvement of independent dealer teams.

But the most impressive news of all had come four months before when Harley had taken the unprecedented step of asking that trade protection tariffs be removed a year early, as 'We no longer need tariff relief to compete with the Japanese.' Buoyed by new Heritage Softail Classic, Electra Glide Sport and Low Rider Custom models, by the year's end they had 47 per cent of the US heavyweight market. In October they bought the rights to the military MT500 from Britain's Armstrong.

Evolution

NAMED the V2 Evolution by Harley, the biggest fault of the latest in Milwaukee's noble line of big twins is the lack of an evocative nickname. After decades of Flatheads, Knuckles, Pans and Shovels, 'Evo' lacks a certain ring (an early suggestion of 'Blockhead' thankfully failed to stick). Yet, despite having a bottom-end whose origins date back to the 61E of 1936, it's an altogether better powerplant than the Shovelhead it replaced.

Compared to the venerable Shovel, which began life 18 years before, the Evo is 20lb (9kg) lighter, producing 10 per cent more horsepower and 15 per cent more torque. Its cylinders retain the 'classic' bore and stroke dimensions of 3.5 x 4.25in (88.8 x 108mm). As with the evolution of Pan- to Shovelhead, the Evo uses much the same bottom end as its (alternator-type) predecessor, but with improved con-rods and an all-alloy top end. The extra power (71bhp at 5000rpm) comes mainly from steeper, straighter ports and higher compression ratios. Much work went into redesigning the lubrication system to prevent the Shovel's notoriously leaky nature. All Evos sport five-speed transmission and, from late '84, a much-improved diaphragm clutch. A year later still Harley made sure their new baby created an impact, with a publicity stunt inspired by the company's 80th birthday celebrations: the plan was to run non-stop for 8000 miles (12,900km) at an average of 80mph (129km/h), with none of the routine servicing a customer's machine would receive. Nor was the test conducted on special one-off machines, but on standard FLT Tour Glides.

Left: The Evo motor might have evolved, but most Harley owners want some natural selection of their own, such as this hot S&S intake set-up. Above right: Harley touring has become big business. Here an Electra Glide and a Road King crest a rise in the Norwegian fjord country. Opposite: You might prefer the warmer climes of Nevada!

At Talladega Speedway in July 1983, the Evolution-engined Tour Glides thundered through the designated 8000 miles, but slightly off the scheduled pace: allowing for mishaps that never occurred, they averaged 85mph (137km/h). The Evo has scarcely looked back.

Modern Times: Nothing Sells Like Nostalgia

HARLEY'S turnaround from near-broke dinosaur to glorious sales success has been one of the miracles of modern motorcycling. There have been four key elements in Harley-Davidson's runaway success over the past decade. The first has been the arrival of the Evolution engine, which was suitably oil-tight and reliable while still being true to its roots. The second was a revolution – not too strong a word – in the way Harleys are made and assembled. This both cut costs and, just as crucially, resulted in a level of build quality hitherto unknown.

Third was a parallel revolution in marketing, promotion and customer satisfaction. The Harley image has been massaged and pushed with great imagination (and ruthlessness: the company is highly protective of its assets). At the core of this has been the worldwide development of the Harley Owners' Group – HOG – which seeks to further inculcate owners into Harley lore. Most H-D dealerships run HOG groups, which arrange everything from hog roasts (naturally) to ride-aways, dances and charity events. The more you live Harley,

the company ethic goes, the more likely you are to stay a free-spending customer. HOG has become the envy of every other motorcycle manufacturer, but is imitated, if at all, only poorly.

The fourth ingredient is sheer good fortune. The most telling Harley attribute is one that no other marque even remotely possesses: Harleys are American. And, in this context, USA also stands for Unique Sales Attribute. It also happens to be the biggest market in the world for big-inch motorcycles.

Harley have played these cards well. By the end of 1987 Harley had 47 per cent of the US superheavyweight market, a figure which had risen to 54 per cent just one year later. President Reagan, conscious of the patriotic feel-good factor, hailed the company as 'an American success story'. And he was right.

Investment and new developments have continued at a steady rate since. 1988 saw more retrotech with the first Springer, a 1200 Sportster, followed by the Fat Boy, Tour Glide and Ultra Glide Ultra Classics. By the early '90s, annual production had reached over 65,000 units, with 20 models accounting for 61 per cent of the US heavyweight market – at a time when Japanese sales were in steep decline, their dealers desperately cutting margins or going out of business altogether. The factory was

Left: New for '97, the Heritage Softail Springer is perhaps the most retro Harley yet, with its Thirties-style springer forks and Forties fenders.

also engaged in an $80 million investment programme. A huge new paint shop finally broke York's production bottleneck, giving a current capacity of around 115,000 machines per year – by far the highest in Harley history.

In 1989 a revamped clothing division – 'MotorClothes' – was launched. This, and the company's burgeoning aftermarket accessories activities, account for a substantial portion of annual profits. It is now possible to buy anything from perfume to souvenir cabinets bedecked with official Harley branding. Although not quite in the Coca-Cola league, it is impossible to overestimate the value of the simple image, 'Harley-Davidson'.

If there is a major concern, it is how Harley

can meet ever-tighter noise and emissions regulations while still remaining true to the essential character of their machines. Despite engines growing bigger, better and more powerful over the years, increasing weight and power-sapping emission regulations mean that speed has scarcely increased. This led to the launch of the first fuel-injected Harleys in 1995. The 'ESPFI' (Electronic Sequential Port Fuel Injection) system is based on a similar Italian Magneti Marelli design used in Ducati V-twins and first appeared on the FLHTC-I Ultra Classic Electra Glide. It makes the engines smoother, cleaner and slightly more powerful. But if pollution restrictions tighten further, as they surely will, the present Evo mill may struggle to respond,

1996 Heritage Softail Classic (above) and the latest Electra Glide Ultra Classic (left), two strikingly different variations on the same 1340cc V-twin theme.

although for the present ESPFI has given the old girl a very useful shot in the arm.

Harley are no doubt working on several solutions. Their most public response has been the VR1000 Superbike racer. Although a V-twin – what else could it be? – it is in every other respects unlike anything Milwaukee has ever produced. Displacing 61cu in (1000cc), and very oversquare (bore 98mm, stroke 66mm), it boasts four valves per cylinder, spins to a giddy 11,000rpm and produces around 140bhp. Even the angle of the 'V', at 60 degrees, is unlike any Harley before.

If the Evolution engine is to be replaced throughout most of the model range, it unlikely to be by something as radical as the VR1000. We may see four-valve heads, possibly overhead camshafts and even liquid-cooling. But it will surely have something of the same unique spirit that Harleys have exuded for generations.

49

Sportsters

EVER SINCE its introduction in 1957, the XL Sportster has been the heart of the Harley-Davidson range. Initial versions were 'Ironheads' of 55cu in (883cc), then the model grew by degrees to 74cu in (1200cc), before a 55-inch (883cc) 'entry-level' stablemate was reintroduced in 1986 with the smallest version of the V² Evolution engine. There are currently five models in the range. Although constantly uprated and refined over the years, Sportsters have always enjoyed unit-construction engines in which the engine and gearbox form an integrated whole.

The line has included many great classics. Possibly the pick of all the Sportsters was the menacing black limited edition XLCR 'cafe racer' unveiled in 1977, although the XR750-like styling of the '82 Anniversary Sportster runs it close. The latter was functionally far superior, thanks to the all-new welded frame introduced that year. Both, needless to say, sprang from the fertile mind of Willie G.

Below: Unlike the Glides and Softails, Sportsters look at their best with the bare minimum of adornment. This handsome example is the XL 1200C Sportster of 1996.

SPECIFICATION	1996 XL 1200C SPORTSTER
ENGINE	1200cc ohv V-twin
POWER	68bhp @ 5500rpm
TORQUE	64lb.ft @ 3500rpm
TRANSMISSION	5-speed
WHEELBASE	59in (1499mm)
FUEL TANK	2.7 gallons (12.3 litres)
WEIGHT (dry)	490lb (222kg)
TOP SPEED	around 100mph (161km/h)

Left: Who needs revs? Ultra-low Sportster Custom churns out a prodigious 64lb.ft of torque at a leisurely 3500rpm.

Both sizes of Sportster share what is essentially the same engine, except that the 1200's bore is 0.5in (12.8mm) greater at 3.5in (88.8mm) (uprating the 883 is a fairly simple job). Peak power is around 52 and 68bhp, respectively. With each engine using a single 40mm constant velocity carb, the larger capacity offers only a little by way of top speed, for each is good for around 103mph (166km/h). The main advantage of the bigger engine lies in the 1200's prodigious torque: around 71lb.ft at 4000rpm, compared to 52 at 4500 for the 883. Overall specifications and dimensions are similar, both having a wheelbase of 60 inches (1524mm) and weighing around 470lb (213kg).

In 1993 the basic 883 became the last Harley to adopt toothed-belt final drive, a smooth, clean, hassle-free alternative to the traditional chain. (Primary drive is by triple-row chain). For 1996 it was the turn of the 1200 to get the treatment, with the introduction of two new models, the XL 1200C (Custom) and XL 1200S (Sport) Sportster. The

Sport featured higher-spec brakes, adjustable rear suspension, a larger tank (at last: the old one was a paltry 1.8 gallons/8.2 litres) and more sporting profile. The Custom is a chrome-lashed styling job making the most of its long, low looks.

While the 'Sportster' label should not be confused with modern race replica machines, the XL has always been the leanest and most purposeful of all Harleys, its brutal no-nonsense lines look best

with a minimum of bolt-on extras. They are, however, raced in special 'one-make' championships on both sides of the Atlantic. Forty V-twins thundering around a race track might not be grand prix racing, but it sure makes a better noise.

Left: Despite the 'Sport' tag, this XL 1200S has no more power and slightly more weight than the custom version. The main differences are in styling and ground clearance.

51

XLH Sportster 883

Below: Good-looking, for sure, with huge pulling power. The lady's quite attractive, too. This 883 Sportster is a direct descendant of the original XL of 1957.

IN TWO short years from 1992, Harley's bargain-basement superbike progressed from being the runt of the Milwaukee litter to become a thoroughly competent machine. There were dozens of detail changes over those two seasons, but two stand out. First came five-speed transmission, then belt final drive. An extra cog transformed the smallest Harley from a buzzy, busy thing into a far more laid-back device, with the bonus of a better shift. The tooth belt drive made it smoother still, with added benefits of low maintenance and cleanliness. The first belts, pioneered by Harley, aroused a degree of suspicion. But they last at least four times as long as a chain, cost about the same, and it is practically unknown for one to fail.

The result is to make the XLH slightly more of what it was always good at – being a lean, spare and handsome means of filling practically all the space between headstock and rear spindle. There are no tassels, no bits that draw their inspiration from a 19th century fairground organ – just plain, single-seated function.

Of course, like all Harleys, the function in question has little to do with sheer speed, handling, or stopping. This is essentially a cut-down cruiser. Its function is to look cool whilst allowing its rider to appreciate, with as little intervening sanitation as possible, the most intimate doings of the internal combustion engine. These doings mainly comprise very large chunks of metal thrashing about, stopping, then thrashing again in the opposite direction. It's a real engine down there, my friend, and not surprisingly it makes a great noise (so good, in fact, that Harley are attempting to copyright it.) If Sportsters have one drawback, it's that tall people can't look very cool on them: they don't fit.

Peak power is around 52bhp at a distinctly unruffled 5500rpm, 2000rpm after maximum torque arrives. Acceleration is brisk rather than vivid, although the ample torque means there's always power on hand. Open the gas at almost any revs and the Sportster lunges forward on an irrepressible wave of power. Without the rubber-mounting available on some larger models, however, engine vibration can be intense at high revs.

Below: Although new variants continue to emerge, the 883 reached its final form with the adoption of belt final drive for the 1993 model year.

SPECIFICATION	XL SPORTSTER 883
ENGINE	53.86cu.in (883cc) ohv V-twin
POWER	52bhp @ 5500rpm
TORQUE	52lb.ft @ 4500rpm
TRANSMISSION	5-speed
WHEELBASE	60.2in (1529mm)
FUEL TANK	2.6 gallons (12.0 litres)
WEIGHT (dry)	488lb (221kg)
TOP SPEED	around 103mph (166km/h)

For genuine Milwaukee hardware, the 883 series represents astonishingly good value. As well as the basic 883, there's the Hugger, a variant dating back to 1979 and so called because it squats even lower to the ground. Sportsters hardly depreciate and, with a bit of care, they all last practically forever. Best of all, 40 years after their introduction they continue to embody the same frill-free virtues as that original '57 XL.

Dyna Glides And Low Riders

ALTHOUGH neither the name nor the concept is new, the Dyna Glides are the newcomers to the Harley-Davidson range. The first model to grace the title was the FXS Low Rider of 1977. Available with either 74- or 80-inch (1200 or 1340cc) powerplant, this was a new type of touring machine, carrying echoes of the choppers which countless enthusiasts had created before. With a two-into-one exhaust system, standard sissy bars and other custom adornments, this was the starting point for budding Easy Riders.

In 1980 the 80-inch FXB Sturgis was added to the family, bringing with it ground-breaking novelties, such as Aramid fibre belt drive in both primary and secondary transmission. Further derivatives available the same year were the FXWG Wide Glide, FXEF Fat Bob and FXS 1200cc Low Rider. Five-speed transmissions first appeared in 1982 on the FXR and FXRS.

The current Dyna Glide range, although taking its visual cues from these models, was transformed by the arrival of a new single backbone frame with the updated Sturgis model of 1991. The Dyna Glide benefited from the same tubework in 1992, and the Dyna Wide Glide one year later. The latter also introduced a new two-point rubber engine mounting system, a substantial improvement over the previous three-point arrangement. Although deceptively simply in appearance, this bestows on the ride an unprecedented level of smoothness.

For 1997 the Dyna family consists of four models: Dyna Super Glide, Dyna Low Rider, Dyna Convertible and Dyna Wide Glide. Although much lighter at 600lb (272kg) than full-on Glide models, all are long and low, with lazy steering. The Super Glide is the base model, with the Dyna Low Rider featuring two front disc brakes and being generally better-equipped. The Convertible carries saddlebags and a neat, quickly-removable screen, whilst the Wide Glide features wide front forks, 'apehanger' 'bars and a 'Fat Bob' tank. Each is powered by the ubiquitous 80-inch (1340cc) V² Evo engine.

Below: This striking black 1991 Sturgis introduced a new frame into the Milwaukee line-up. Its clever rubber-mounting systems later graced the Dyna Glide models.

Left and below: The '93 Dyna Wide Glide combined the new twin-point rubber mounting of the previous Sturgis/ Dyna models with widely-splayed front forks (hence the Wide Glide tag). Other standard custom items included a 21 inch front wheel, factory 'ape-hanger' handlebars, a 'tucked-in tail light', and 'air-foil directionals'. Less obviously, the new 'Fat Bob' tank is not only two pints bigger than before, but is now made in one piece — much more convenient. In common with all 1340cc '93 models, a new engine breather system cleans up the plumbing around the air cleaner housing.

SPECIFICATION	FXDWG DYNA WIDE GLIDE
ENGINE	1340cc ohv V-twin
POWER	69bhp @ 5400rpm
TORQUE	70lb.ft @ 3000rpm
TRANSMISSION	5-speed
WHEELBASE	66in (1679mm)
FUEL TANK	4.3 gallons (19.7 litres)
WEIGHT (dry)	598lb (271kg)
TOP SPEED	around 108mph (174km/h)

55

THE MILWAUKEE NAME GAME

Harley model codes may appear bewildering, but the cipher is fairly simple. All recent Harleys start with one of these combinations of letters, which denote certain engine and chassis combinations (more or less):

XL/XLH: Sportster range, comprising solidly-mounted 55cu in (883cc) and 74cu in (1200cc) engines. The prefix dates back to the original 55-inch (883cc) XL Sportster of 1957. The 'H' originally stood for 'hot'.

FX: models with 80cu in (1340cc) Evo engines, with extra letters to denote chassis type:
FXR/FXLR: 'sport' chassis: Low Riders, Sport Glide and Super Glide, rubber-mounted engines;
FXD: Dyna Glides, with part-forged 'Sturgis' chassis and rubber-mounted engines;
FXST: Softails, engine not rubber-mounted.

FL: heavyweight Glides, all with rubber-mounted 80cu in (1340cc) Evo engines. (Except where 'FL' is followed by 'ST' which denotes a Softail broadly styled after the 1949 Hydra-Glide – Fat Boy and Heritage Softail.)

Then you get suffixes to the prefixes:

B   Bad Boy, formerly Daytona or belt final drive

C   Custom or Classic

Conv 'Convertible': removable windshield

D   Daytona

F   Fat Boy

H   Electra Glide (forks-mounted fairing), except where the 'H' is preceded by 'XL'

I   Fuel injection

L, R or LR
     Low Rider. R also indicates Road King

-SP Sport, as in FXRS-SP Low Rider Sport Edition

ST   Softail: rear suspension that doesn't look like suspension

S   Springer, as in FXSTS Springer Softail or Sport, as in FLHS Electra Glide Sport

T   frame-mounted fairing, as in FLT Tour Glide

U   Ultra, as in Ultra Classic

WG   Wide Glide

Thus, XLHSTSTC-SP denotes a Sports version of the Custom edition, Softail-chassised Sportster with a Springer front end, frame-mounted fairing, and solidly-mounted engine of either 55cu in or 74cu in (883cc or 1200cc). Thankfully, Harley has yet to build such a monstrosity.

Simple, huh?

Above: Some acronyms are more familiar than others. 'USA' stands for the place where Harley-Davidsons are proud to be made. Opposite: variations on Dyna's theme: Wide Glide (top left), Low Rider (top right) and the latest incarnation of the historic Super Glide.

Retro-Tech: Softails

THE SOFTAILS are the style kings of the Harley-Davidson range. 'Retro-tech' means something modern but executed and styled in a recognisably 'classic' way. No one is quite sure when the label was first coined, or who was responsible, but the machine which first warranted it was the seminal Softail of 1984. This was doubly fitting, as not only was this striking new model's hardtail appearance quite novel, but so was its engine: the Softail was the first Harley powered by the all-new, long-awaited 80-inch (1340cc) V² Evolution engine.

To achieve the hardtail illusion, Harley engineers designed a massive triangulated rear swinging fork, with twin shock absorbers mounted beneath where they were hidden from normal view. The clean overall lines of the machine emphasized the elegant sweep from head stock to rear wheel spindle, heightening the hardtail effect. Visually, however, the cues lay way back in 1949 with the Hydra-Glide, the first Harley model with telescopic front forks. Large-diameter bright metal fork shrouds further mimicked the period style. If any modern motorcycle belonged parked outside a Fifties American diner, the throwback Softail was surely it.

This inspired piece of post-modern design was a huge, instant success. Although not the most practical of Harleys, Softails are certainly the most eye-catching and the most prized. Since '84, the Softail range has expanded. 1985 brought the first of a distinguished line of Heritage Softails, a line which for many adherents reached its peak in the delicious 1993 FLSTN Heritage Softail Nostalgia.

Meanwhile Harley's stylists discovered even more retro-potential by looking back even farther. 1988 – or was it '42? – brought the first Springer Softail, with girder-type suspension with exposed springs, reminiscent of a pre-war big twin.

There are now no less than six models in the Softail range: Softail Custom, Bad Boy, Springer Softail, Fat Boy, Heritage Softail Classic and the new Heritage Springer Softail. The latter, reminiscent of a '48 Panhead, is a retro-tech tour de force. As Harley put it: 'loaded with chrome and leather, the Heritage

Opposite: A Heritage Softail Classic and Low Rider cruise in the twilight. As well as being the height of fashion, both are capable long-haul machines.

Springer Softail screams nostalgia . . . fringed-and-embossed leather . . . tractor-style seat . . . leather fringed valance embossed with a basket-weave pattern and accented with conchos . . . leather fringed saddlebags . . . dual-fishtail mufflers . . . whitewall tires . . . floating front fender . . . retro-'40s tombstone taillight . . .' Over the top, certainly, but delicious.

All Softails boast 80cu in (1340cc) five-speed engines with duplex chain primary drive and belt final drive. All roll on 16-inch rear wheels, with the first three having a 21-inch front, the rest a 16-incher. And all, of course, share the same frame, with Harley's clever rear suspension, utilizing paired gas-filled shock absorbers hidden beneath the belly of the bike. Power in all cases is 69bhp at 5000rpm, with a prodigious 76lb.ft of torque at 3500rpm.

The other differences between them are mainly in the detail – spoked or disc wheels, whitewall or conventional tyres, extra running lights, splashes of chrome trim. Both Heritages, however, sport leather saddlebags as standard, with the Classic also offering a windshield. This may seem underwhelming to riders weaned on the glut of exotic new sports models pouring each year from Japan. But Harley fans prefer the more timeless, dependable attractions of real American iron. And who can deny the understated elegance of the Fat Boy's uncluttered lines?

Above: More chrome, anybody?

SPECIFICATION	HERITAGE SOFTAIL CLASSIC
ENGINE	1340cc ohv V-twin
POWER	69bhp @ 5400rpm
TORQUE	70lb.ft @ 3000rpm
TRANSMISSION	5-speed
WHEELBASE	64in (1623mm)
FUEL TANK	3.5 gallons (15.9 litres)
WEIGHT (dry)	698lb (317kg)
TOP SPEED	around 105mph (169km/h)